COVER TO COVER

BIBLE **STUDY**

7 SESSIONS FOR SMALL GROUP
AND PERSONAL USE

1 Peter

GOOD REASONS FOR HOPE

CWR

Dave Edwins

Contents

4 Introduction

7 Week 1
Good Reasons for Hope

13 Week 2
Living as God's Holy People

19 Week 3
Chosen to Belong

25 Week 4
Now Give In!

31 Week 5
Don't Let Suffering Take You by Surprise

37 Week 6
Live Wisely

43 Week 7
Ready to Serve Like Jesus

49 Leader's Notes

Introduction

There is a story told of an elderly German philosopher who was found by a policeman sitting on a park bench. The policeman challenged him with two questions, 'Who are you?' and 'What are you doing?' to which the philosopher replied 'I wish to God I knew!' In today's world there are many who are unsure of who they are and how they fit into the world. Perhaps they have been displaced by war, conflict or unrest. Some have become refugees fleeing the ravages of malnutrition, while others are desperately seeking their roots in order to have anchor points in their lives.

As Peter writes this letter to Christians living in the Roman provinces of what we know now as northern Turkey, he is aware that his Christian brothers and sisters are struggling to come to terms with who they are in Christ and to whom they belong (see the confidence of Paul in Acts 27:23). Throughout the letter Peter encourages these Christians to remember that they are refugees in a hostile environment (1:1) and despite the outside pressure of their pagan neighbours, they belong to God because they have been bought with a price (1:19; 3:18). Here in the midst of uncertainty they can find security in who they are in Christ and in the promise of an imperishable future inheritance, secured by Christ's resurrection from the dead.

Many of those being addressed were slaves or household servants and someone has commented that at this time in the Roman Empire you either were a slave or you owned a slave. A conservative estimate suggests that there were at least sixty million slaves in the world of the first century. Peter's choice of words indicates that he is writing to all workers – including house workers who may have been paid employees as well as slaves. It was tough for some who were believers to maintain a witness when subject to cruel or tyrannical masters.

Over 200 years ago William Wilberforce and his friends worked tirelessly to bring an end to the slave trade. Later the struggles of the American Civil War largely brought an end to slavery in the Americas. In our twenty-first century, we must still be alert to the dangers of hidden slavery; workers are exploited in sweat shops, young women and men are traded for the sex industry and others lose their employment due to the practices of unscrupulous bosses. How will we play our part in seeking to bring this kind of exploitation to an end and in setting people free?

A key theme for Peter is how to handle unjust suffering. Generally Peter is directing his attention to the suffering of those who are employed or enslaved. He is not speaking about suffering caused by illness, although there are principles which may be applied in those situations too. The inevitability of suffering, for those who love and follow Christ, is clearly expressed together with the possibilities of enjoying His grace in the midst of the tough times. There is no immunity for believers from the ravages of persecution – as Paul says to Timothy, 'In fact, everyone who wants to live a godly life in Christ Jesus will be persecuted' (2 Tim. 3:12). Early persecution came mainly from the Jewish authorities but it is likely that Peter was preparing these Christians for the inevitability of a clamp down from the Roman Emperors who demanded that they be worshipped as gods. The apostle was also keen to encourage these beleaguered Christians to live out their faith in such a way that they provided an eloquent witness to the power of Christ. How often do we retreat into the comfort and safety of our Christian family or church group when the pressure is turned up? We are urged in 1 Peter 3:15 to always be prepared to give the reason for the hope we have in Christ.

Chapters 2 and 3 contain a very significant section devoted to the area of relationships. How do you live a respectful life as a slave when you are being abused and beaten by your master? What responsibilities do we have as citizens towards those who are in authority over us? Then Peter directs his teaching towards how husbands and wives may live in harmony. This relationship was complicated by the fact that many Christian wives had unbelieving husbands. Many of these issues are still on the agenda of the Church today.

A number of commentators note that this letter was possibly designed as a discipleship tool for young Christians or even formed part of a baptismal sermon. Whatever its original usage, this short letter provided much encouragement for first century believers and also for us too, in terms of living in 'the true grace of God' (5:12) and standing firm in the storms of life. We must not miss the fact, too, that throughout Peter points us to our future hope. We may live confidently because the day of Christ's return in glory is near and that means we should get prepared by living in that hope right now.

WEEK 1

Good Reasons for Hope

Opening Icebreaker

Think back to your childhood and share about a time when you clung on to a hope which you were confident would be fulfilled. Perhaps this was to do with a family holiday or an anticipated gift.

Bible Readings

- 1 Peter 1:1–12
- Job 17:10–16
- Psalm 33:16–22
- Isaiah 40:28–31
- Romans 8:37–39
- Hebrews 6:13–20

Opening Our Eyes

In keeping with the custom of the times, the author begins his letter by identifying who he is: when you examine the evidence from the writing you realise that you are in the presence of an eyewitness of the life of Jesus. In 2:23 we are reminded of the way that Jesus went to the cross with no retaliation and in 5:1 the writer declares himself to have been a witness to the sufferings of Jesus. In chapter 5 a call is issued to church leaders to be 'shepherds of God's flock' which seems to echo back to the scene on the Galilean beach in John 21 when Peter was recommissioned to be a shepherd – 'feed my sheep' (John 21:17).

In the opening verse the writer establishes his credentials, declaring that he is Peter, once known as Simon, who, having experienced the amazing grace of Jesus and been a witness to His resurrection, has now been set apart to be 'a sent one'. Much as an ambassador is sent from one country to be its spokesperson in another, an apostle is one sent with the job of representing Jesus to an unbelieving world.

With a clear pastoral intent, Peter encourages these hard pressed believers to remember that they have been chosen by their all powerful, three-in-one God (v2). Notice the Trinitarian formula used here: the Father who chooses us, the Holy Spirit who helps us and Jesus Christ who cleanses us, in order that we might live in obedience to God. Here is an excellent reason to be hopeful in tough times – we belong to Him.

It seems that hope is in short supply in our struggling world, just as it was in the first century world of Peter. So firstly, he invites these struggling Christians to look forward, and he shares the good news that there is

an inheritance waiting for them which is absolutely
certain and true. They have already begun this 'brand-
new life' (*The Message*) and despite their pain, they are
secure in God's safekeeping. This hope is built on the
secure foundation of the resurrection of Christ and is
thus guaranteed. As Edmund Clowney points out 'Not
only is our inheritance kept for us; we are kept for our
inheritance.'[1]

Secondly, well aware of their trials and tribulations, Peter
encourages them to stand firm in the present, because
they are safe in God's almighty power (v5). The word
used here in the Greek indicates that they are being
guarded or shielded, a metaphor that was commonly
used in the Psalms – see Psalms 7:10, 18:2, 28:7, 119:114
and 144:2. This was a cause for rejoicing even though
circumstances seemed to demand a different response.

Thirdly, they needed to remember the past because it
is evident that God had already planned and prepared
for them to be secure in times of trial. The prophets of
old had predicted the sufferings of the Messiah, which
would be followed by glory. This principle is important
to learn: suffering often precedes glory. Paul comments
in Philippians 3:10 that the power or glory of the
resurrection life is often accompanied by suffering:
it was for our Lord and it will be for many of us, too.

Discussion Starters

1. Which verse really spoke to you in the reading?

   _____
   _____
   _____
   _____
   _____

2. How does the introduction to the letter help you understand the working of the three persons of God?

   _____
   _____
   _____
   _____
   _____

3. Think about the story of Peter in the Gospels and Acts. How can you trace the working of grace in his life? Then think about your life and share what you have experienced of this.

   _____
   _____
   _____
   _____
   _____

4. Look again at the reasons Peter gives these Christians for not losing hope. When you are tempted to throw in the towel, how might these reasons encourage you to keep going?

   _____
   _____
   _____
   _____
   _____

5. Read Job chapter 1 and 17:10–16 again and consider the journey that Job went on after the events of chapter 1. How did he find hope amidst the tragedy and the constant unhelpful advice of his friends?

_____

_____

_____

_____

_____

6. What are the results of genuine faith (1 Pet. 1:7–9)?

_____

_____

_____

_____

7. How important is the resurrection of Jesus to you? What difference does knowing that Jesus is alive make to your daily life?

_____

_____

_____

_____

_____

8. How joyful are you feeling today? Discuss together what helps you to rejoice even when things are tough.

_____

_____

_____

_____

_____

Personal Application

In what ways are Christians suffering for their faith in the world today? What should be our response to a friend who is overlooked for promotion or demoted for being truthful? How will we get our hands dirty in supporting those who struggle?

Perhaps you could research and gather information in order to pray more effectively for those persecuted for their faith. As you pray, seek God afresh and ask Him to fill them and you with His joy whatever the circumstances.

Peter was an ambassador for Jesus and we too are called to be witnesses (Acts 1:8). How are you doing in this? My challenge is always whether my life mirrors my words or whether I have become like the 'resounding gong or a clanging cymbal' of 1 Corinthians 13:1.

Seeing Jesus in the Scriptures

Jesus came to earth knowing the plan of His Father and well aware of the prophets' writings which clearly indicated the manner of His death. Yet He was still prepared to undertake the amazing rescue plan that we know as salvation. Jesus endured the cruel suffering of the cross, completely undeserved, so that we might experience forgiveness and the joy of a new relationship with Him. What hope this brings and how it draws out my praise for a Saviour who loves me unconditionally and who will never stop loving me. I love the words of the late Brennan Manning in *The Ragamuffin Gospel*: 'My deepest awareness of myself is that I am deeply loved by Jesus Christ and I have done nothing to earn it or deserve it.'

Notes
[1]Edmund Clowney, *The Message of 1 Peter* (BST: IVP, 1989) p49

WEEK 2

Living as God's Holy People

Opening Icebreaker

Imagine you are at a cash machine (ATM) and in response to your request for a small amount of cash, the machine gives you twice the amount of money you requested. How do you respond? Do you furtively put it in your purse or take it to the nearest police station? Examine the motivation for your decision.

Bible Readings

- 1 Peter 1:13–2:3
- Leviticus 19:1–2
- Isaiah 6:1–7
- 2 Corinthians 1:12–14
- Philippians 1:27–30
- 1 Thessalonians 4:7

Opening Our Eyes

This next section begins with a 'Therefore', demanding
that we look back to previous discussion. In chapter 1,
Peter pointed out to these young Christians that despite
their difficult circumstances, they have a hope that is
rooted in the past and confirmed in the present, with
an expectation of a future glorious inheritance. This is
further cemented in the fact that Jesus has died and been
resurrected. In the light of that good news, the apostle
instructs them to live in a way that would honour Christ.
The tone of the writing changes at this point from gentle
pleadings to direct commands. You have come to faith;
now live in obedience to the One who set you free.

We have a role to play in living like Jesus and we are
invited to prepare our minds (v13). The picture is one
of gathering together a garment and tucking it into a
belt, so that it doesn't impede progress; today we might
say 'roll up your sleeves'. The importance of the mind
is never played down in the New Testament (Rom. 8:6;
12:2). A mind under the authority of Christ is essential
in holy living. Paul is a great example of a man totally
intoxicated with Christ but able to use his intellect to be
an effective witness; which was what perplexed Festus in
Acts 26:24. C.E.B. Cranfield declares that there is 'a call
to the strenuous but exhilarating adventure of trying to
understand ever more and more deeply the gospel'.[1]

The fear that is referred to in verse 17 is not cringing fear
but rather a worshipful response to a holy God, mindful
always that He is our all-powerful and all-knowing
heavenly Father. As we consider the cost of our salvation,
we realise that it was not paid for by human finance but
with the price of the precious blood of Jesus. Borrowing
the imagery of the slave market, Peter reminds his

brothers and sisters that a far greater price had been paid for them.

Again, in verse 22, Peter acknowledges the part that the believer plays in living a wholesome Christian life. The sense here is that because you have submitted to the truth of the gospel and probably been through the waters of baptism, the reference to 'purified' might indicate that you are now able to love with sincerity. It is likely that Peter recalled what Jesus said in his final instructions and prayer for the disciples; they were to love one another and live in unity so that the unbelieving world might know the reality of Christ (John 17:23). What a powerful witness it is when His people 'love one another deeply, from the heart' (1 Pet. 1:22). I wonder how this might have impacted these household slaves or servants and reverberated to their masters and mistresses? There is, too, in the Greek, a sense that one needed to stretch out or make strenuous effort, suggesting that this love will make big demands on us. The love called for here is tough love; love that goes beyond a mere profession.

Peter issues a call to action in 2:1–3, to deal with what Paul Rees calls the germs which quickly infect groups of people living in relationship.[2] The first of these is ill-will or malice, then deviousness or deceit, followed by insincerity or hypocrisy, envy and finally defamation or slander. Allow these germs to develop and Christian fellowship will be destroyed. Instead Peter encourages his friends to earnestly desire the godly sustenance of God's Word.

Discussion Starters

1. How can you roll up your intellectual sleeves and be more informed in your faith?

_____

_____

_____

_____

_____

2. Think about holiness and ask yourself how different you are from those around you who do not know Jesus yet. What are the areas in which you particularly need the power of Christ to work?

_____

_____

_____

_____

_____

3. Peter uses the words 'exiles' and 'foreigners' in verse 1 and verse 17. What do you think this means in the context of the letter and how could it affect the way you live?

_____

_____

_____

_____

_____

4. Why does Peter encourage us to live in reverent fear (v17)? What is healthy fear and how will it affect you?

_____

_____

_____

_____

_____

5. Peter quotes a lot from the Old Testament; there are more quotes in this letter than any other New Testament book with the exception of Romans. Have you tried to memorise the Bible and what help has it been to you?

_____

_____

_____

_____

_____

6. How can you develop in loving others? Is there anyone with whom you have difficulty? How are you going to love them sincerely? What practical steps can you take?

_____

_____

_____

_____

_____

7. None of us likes to think that the 'germs' of 2:1 are affecting us. Allow God to put His finger on anything with which He is unhappy. Discuss how best to deal with these destructive 'germs'.

_____

_____

_____

_____

_____

8. What is spiritual milk? Are you getting your daily requirement? Share with the group things that help you to feed on the 'pure spiritual milk' of God.

_____

_____

_____

_____

Personal Application

What does the word 'holiness' mean to you? Maybe you imagine a group of religious zealots living in isolation from the world, seeking not to be contaminated by worldly pleasures. Perhaps you have been labelled at work because of your unwillingness to conform or because of your faithful witness. How can you live a holy life and not be considered weird? The call is to be faithful to Christ and allow His life to shine out through you. What does this mean in practice in daily living? Are you spending time in company with Jesus and allowing Him to transform your life?

Seeing Jesus in the Scriptures

Seeking to live like Jesus seems impossible. We see His holiness and recognise the authenticity of His lifestyle. We long to be like Him, so we pray and seek God for change in the way that we behave, yet find ourselves constantly returning to the cross for forgiveness. It is not by our efforts that change will be accomplished but by an infusion of His life into ours. The work of salvation has already been completed: now the crucified, risen Lord wants to nourish us with the spiritual milk of the Word. It will always be a battle, as we know from Paul's writing to the Romans in chapter 7. The brilliant news, however, is that we can be more than conquerors despite the forces of darkness which are lined up against us and that 'absolutely *nothing* can get between us and God's love because of the way that Jesus our Master has embraced us' (Rom. 8:39 *The Message*).

Notes
[1]C.E.B. Cranfield, *1 & 2 Peter and Jude* (SCM, 1960) p47
[2]P.S. Rees, *Triumphant in Trouble – Studies in 1 Peter* (London: Marshall: Morgan & Scott, 1962)

WEEK 3

Chosen to Belong

Opening Icebreaker

Just suppose that you have just been adopted into a royal family and your home is now a palace. What rights and privileges would you most enjoy?

Bible Readings

- 1 Peter 2:4–12
- Isaiah 41:8–10
- Romans 14:7–8
- 1 Corinthians 6:19–20
- 2 Corinthians 5:14–15
- Galatians 5:24–25
- Ephesians 1:3–14

Opening Our Eyes

In 1505 a young sculptor in Florence was invited to carve a block of Carrara marble known as 'The Giant'. It had lain idle for nearly 100 years after the bungled attempt of a previous sculptor left it severely flawed. He spent several months looking at it and making sketches; three years later, he unveiled the mighty statue we know as 'David'. The sculptor was, of course, Michelangelo. Peter reminds us (2:4) that Jesus was also rejected by his own people because He did not fit expectations of a Messiah, despite the fact that He was chosen by His Father as the chief cornerstone. To those in the early Christian community who acknowledged His leadership, Jesus was a treasured foundation stone.

The good news for those who followed Jesus was that they, too, could have confidence that they were chosen and accepted by God; living stones being put together into a building. How do you understand the word 'church'? For many it is the building which they attend to worship God, but Peter sees it much more as a group of people of all shapes and sizes being built into a 'spiritual house' (v5). The foundation of any building is crucial if it is to stand and remain strong, and the stone rejected by others is the chief cornerstone.

An important note sounded by Peter negates any idea that these Christians were second class citizens, for they were part of a community built upon Jesus. Today, too, many struggle with feelings of inadequacy, but Peter helps them to understand that they are a chosen people (v9), belonging to God. Again, there is a reminder that a redemption price has been paid in Jesus' death and although they may still have belonged to an earthly master, they needed to understand that they were God's treasured possession.

Several word pictures are used to describe this new community. Peter says that they are stones in the common building (vv4–8), priests in the common worship centre (vv5,9), and citizens of the common nation (vv9–10). The picture springs to mind of dry stone walling, used in various parts of the UK. The stones used are never exactly the same because they are quarried. Yet the skill of the craftsperson is to fit them together so that they form a cohesive and strong wall. In the church of Christ we come in many unique sizes and shapes as living stones, but built together we are strong, clearly demonstrating the craftsmanship of the master builder.

An important concept to grasp was that they were no longer dependent on a priesthood that had the sole privilege of appearing in God's presence – they were now a 'holy priesthood'. Their sacrifices of service and dedication were just as acceptable as those previously offered in the temple, because they were now offered through Jesus.

If we are foreigners and exiles in this world (words repeated in v11), then we are citizens of a different kingdom and we are now people of God (Exod. 19:1–6). These privileges are not given to us to become self-absorbed, but to share with the world everything that God has done for us (v9). We are a vital part of God's eternal plan to bring His good news to those who, as yet, have never experienced His love. The final verses (vv11–12), remind us that the good news of the gospel needs to be shared from lives that are clean and that honour Christ.

Discussion Starters

1. What would you expect to observe in the life of a person who claimed to be a 'living stone'?

_____

_____

_____

_____

2. Read The Parable of the Tenants in Matthew 21:33–46 and Psalm 118:22 to find some commentary on this passage in 1 Peter 2. How precious is Jesus to you? How have you found Him to be the rock in your life?

_____

_____

_____

_____

_____

3. Why do you think Peter quotes so much from the Old Testament? Do you spend much time reading it and is it preached upon much in your church?

_____

_____

_____

_____

_____

4. Think through the implications of being part of a 'royal priesthood', a 'holy nation', a 'spiritual house' and a 'chosen people'. Does this bring encouragement or feelings of inadequacy?

_____

_____

_____

_____

_____

5. What are the battles that you struggle with and what are the secrets of winning the victory?

_____

_____

_____

_____

_____

6. It is very easy to become critical of the local church and to observe lots of shortcomings. Spend some time as a group sharing recent blessings and then turn them into praise.

_____

_____

_____

_____

_____

7. Discuss how you can be both an 'exile' and 'foreigner' in the world and still be an effective witness for Christ.

_____

_____

_____

_____

_____

8. What does it mean for you to know that you have been chosen to be part of His family?

_____

_____

_____

_____

_____

Personal Application

Building with living stones is a hazardous occupation, but our God has many years of experience in the business of shaping those stones so that they can play their part in His family. Where are you finding His chisel at work in your life right now? Are you able to allow Him the opportunity to shape you, even though it might be painful at times? Check out the sketch performed by the Skit Guys called 'God's Chisel'.[1]

How about the battles that you fight with temptation? Draw on His mighty strength to help you overcome, and submit to the Holy Spirit, who wants to live out the life of Jesus in you. The allegory that Jesus gave His disciples in John 15 might be helpful: as branches we need to stay firmly attached to the vine so that the goodness of the vine might flow through us.

Seeing Jesus in the Scriptures

Peter declares that Jesus was rejected and ignored by His own people. Today He is still deemed unfashionable and irrelevant by many in our world, yet His grace is at work seeking those who have become detached or lost from God. The intention of God His Father is to demonstrate to a watching world that it is deeply loved and to show His glorious grace. The vehicle He intends to use is the Church, the body of Christ; in other words you and me and all those who know Jesus as their Saviour and Lord. What an amazing plan! How will you play your part in living in such a way that Jesus is seen and that His grace is clearly displayed?

Notes
[1] www.skitguys.com/videos/item/gods-chisel

WEEK 4

Now Give In!

Opening Icebreaker

The Union of which you are a member has decided to strike. How do you react to this news and how does this challenge your deeply held Christian beliefs?

Bible Readings

- 1 Peter 2:13–25; 3:1–7
- Romans 12:1–3
- Romans 13:1–7
- Ephesians 5:22–6:9
- Colossians 3:18–4:1
- Philemon 8–21

Opening Our Eyes

Submission is not a very fashionable word today, but Peter shows in this section of the letter that there are three particular areas where it is important that Christians understand their responsibilities and the need to submit.

The key verse is 2:16 which the NLT translates as 'you are free, yet you are God's slaves'. Other human relationships fall into place when we resolve the issue of who is number one in our lives. It is evident from other New Testament writers that they considered that having been redeemed by Jesus, they owed Him everything and they lived under His leadership. So Paul writes to the Corinthian Christians (1 Cor. 6:19–20) reminding them that they are not their own because they have been purchased at the price of Christ's death. This would resonate with those with firsthand experience as servants and slaves.

Firstly, Peter addressed submission to rulers and authorities. There is certainly no call for uprising or anarchy here. We are encouraged to see those who govern us as tools in God's hand, although they only have authority as far as He allows it. There needs to be order, otherwise life becomes chaotic and it is impossible to live effectively. Laws are established so that things function in a good way. There are privileges as well as responsibilities of being citizens of a nation. However, there are differences between then and now: under Rome's authority 'subjugation' was a key word, whereas we are more likely to talk in terms of 'co-operation' because we have an opportunity to participate in government. Peter urged his readers to live with respect even when they felt they were mistreated, because that testified to the grace of God and silenced false accusation (vv13–17).

Secondly, submissive behaviour and respect needed to be shown towards masters and mistresses, even when they were unkind or inconsiderate. If you are being treated unfairly, your response could easily lead to hatred or rebellion. That is where the grace of God should kick in and the attitude of Jesus should shine through. Peter encourages his friends to look at the example of Jesus (vv21–23); even if they are beaten unjustly, He is near to help. It is helpful to note in verse 25 that there are two Greek words used to indicate the work of Jesus now on our behalf. He is the Shepherd who found us when we were wandering and the Guardian who watches our every footstep to protect us.

Finally, (3:1–7), marital relationship is considered. When reading this we need to remember that in the Roman Empire women were regarded as 'things', with very few rights. Both verses 1 and 7 begin with, 'in the same way', drawing our attention to the example of Jesus that concludes the previous chapter. How did Jesus handle suffering? He 'entrusted himself' or submitted Himself to His Father's will. So the call is for husbands as well as wives to submit themselves to each other, echoing the instruction of Paul in Ephesians 5:21 to 'Submit to one another out of reverence for Christ'. It is thought likely that many of these women were married to unbelieving husbands and the instruction to honour and respect their spouse was crucial if they wanted to see them won for Christ. We need to remember that we are heirs together of God's 'gracious gift of life' and as mutual respect and partnership grows, our prayer life becomes unhindered and God is honoured, too.

Discussion Starters

1. What is the role of God-given authorities? How should we react to unjust laws being passed in our parliament or ruling assembly?

2. Do you think that you show proper respect to everyone (v17)? What areas of your life do you need to review? Why is it important for our Christian witness?

3. How do people in your country suffer in their work situations because they own the name of Christ? Spend some time praying for those under pressure to conform.

4. Consider the sufferings of Christ and talk about the lessons you can learn from them for your daily living.

5. You have been asked to mentor a young couple contemplating marriage. What would you want to say to them from this passage?
Compare Ephesians 5:21–33 and Colossians 3:18–4:1.

_____

_____

_____

_____

_____

6. What do you think Peter meant by saying that wives were the 'weaker partner' (v7)?

_____

_____

_____

_____

_____

7. What is your description of 'beautiful' when applied to a person? How does that view match up to Peter's view in 3:3–4?

_____

_____

_____

_____

8. What hinders your prayer life?

_____

_____

_____

_____

Personal Application

Many of us are content with the civil authorities that rule over us. We have the chance to participate in governing, perhaps with a local council or school board. How will you guard your attitudes in regard to living submissively and maintain a healthy respect for those who have authority over you? In an increasingly secular society we need to be able to help people understand the importance of Christian values and their contribution to effective life. Ask God for a fresh infilling of His Spirit so that you can make your own special contribution to the society in which you live.

Seeing Jesus in the Scriptures

The sufferings of Christ as described by Peter are a great example for us when we are experiencing struggles and opposition. Re-examine His attitude and read again the powerful words of Philippians 2:5–11, letting them challenge you afresh. Jesus suffered not just the physical pain but also the mental agony of separation from His Father, the first time in all eternity that Jesus had experienced such anguish. Jesus entrusted Himself into His Father's hands and we can draw on that strength, too. Circumstances may challenge us as they did Jesus, but now that He has broken death's power we too can experience His mighty, overcoming power.

WEEK 5

Don't Let Suffering Take You by Surprise

Opening Icebreaker

Discuss together any situations when you have suffered for your faith. Did it take you by surprise and how did you handle it?

Bible Readings

- 1 Peter 3:8–22; 4:12–19
- Isaiah 53
- Romans 8:17–21
- 1 Corinthians 12:26
- 2 Corinthians 11:23–33
- Philippians 3:10–11

Opening Our Eyes

In Peter's mind, suffering was an integral part of salvation; an inevitability if you were a true follower of Christ. He wants to point out that when suffering comes, those who name Christ's name need to be united and speak with one voice.

There are five important characteristics that should be part of our daily living (vv8–9). Firstly, harmony or like-mindedness. Literally it means to think the same way about things and it calls us again to exercise our minds (Phil. 2:5). Secondly sympathy, which encourages us to enter into the needs and concerns of another and support them. Thirdly the command is to exercise brotherly love, loving others just as we have been loved by Jesus. Fourthly, be compassionate, which is a grace evident in our Lord Jesus and which comes from deep within us. We have received the amazing love of Christ (2:24; 3:18) and the call is for us to exercise similar tender care in our dealings with others. Lastly, a word that was despised by the culture of the first century, namely humility. C.S. Lewis is reputed to have observed that it is not thinking less of yourself but thinking of yourself less. When lived out, these five blessings enable us to be a blessing to others even in the midst of trials.

Looking at suffering in the life of a Christian we see that it is a normal expectation, thus Peter writes in 3:9 that it is part of our calling and it will ultimately lead to our blessing. While we endure the hostility and cruelty of others we have no need to fear, but rather look for opportunities to share the reality of our faith. Again, Peter joins up the thinking, encouraging us to live lives which display the glory of Christ and then be prepared to give reasons for the hope which resides within.

There is a return here to the facts of the suffering of

Christ. There is no doubt that He died and it was not just mere imagination (v18). His death on the cross was necessary in order that our disobedience and rebellion could be dealt with; this moves us from alienation and separation into membership of His family, all of this being confirmed by His resurrection from the dead (vv18, 21).

Peter wraps up chapter 3 with one of the most difficult passages in the New Testament (vv19–20): one of the most popular interpretations is that between His death and resurrection, Jesus went to a place where fallen angels are imprisoned and proclaimed to them His victory and their defeat (see 2 Peter 2:4). Get hold of a good commentary[1] and review the arguments. It could be that Peter includes these verses to demonstrate the victory of Christ over demonic powers because these folk detected the enemy's work in their trials and suffering. They needed to know that Jesus had triumphed and that although the lion might roar, he was defeated.

Finally (4:12–19), Peter reminds his readers that being part of Christ's family will inevitably lead to trials. So they are called not to be surprised (v12) but to remember that they are involved in the sufferings of Christ. They are instructed not to be ashamed (v16) because they are participants in the family of Christ and bear His name. Finally, Peter calls them to remain faithful (v19), confident in the keeping and sustaining power of God. In a far greater way than someone putting money in a bank trusting that it will remain secure, we may have complete confidence in our faithful Creator (v19).

Discussion Starters

1. How can we live in harmony as followers of Christ? What help can we give to each other?

_____

_____

_____

_____

_____

2. What does it mean to be humble today?

_____

_____

_____

_____

_____

3. Often fear can overwhelm us when we least expect it. What encouragement would you give to a friend who is troubled in this way?

_____

_____

_____

_____

_____

4. Read Isaiah 53 again and consider the predicted sufferings of Christ. How does this speak into your life today?

_____

_____

_____

_____

_____

5. Share together ways of taking opportunities for speaking of Jesus. Perhaps some might like to practise telling their story in one minute.

_____

_____

_____

_____

_____

6. How do you view baptism? What is its purpose for the believer? How did God bless you when you were baptised?

_____

_____

_____

_____

7. It is easy to say rejoice when you are going through trials and suffering, but practically speaking, how do you actually do that?

_____

_____

_____

_____

8. How have you discovered the dependability of God at various times in your life?

_____

_____

_____

_____

Personal Application

In chapter 2:1 we considered the damage done by 'five germs' that often afflict groups of Christian people. Here in chapter 3:8 we have some antidotes or encouragements to behave in a totally counter-cultural way. Examine the two lists and consider the areas that you need to work on with the Holy Spirit's aid.

Although what the suffering Peter primarily speaks about is to do with the struggles of slaves and their unjust masters, how might these passages help someone who is stressed by the ravages of long-term illness? Is there someone you know who needs encouragement today?

Seeing Jesus in the Scriptures

Whilst ministering on earth, Jesus tried to prepare His disciples for His impending death (Mark 8:31–9:1). It seems that they never really grasped the truth that He was trying to teach them. Not only His death but also His resurrection took them by surprise. When the women returned from the tomb on that first Easter morning the inclination was to disbelieve their story (Luke 24:11). Note the number of references that Peter makes to the resurrection of Jesus in this letter and evaluate the importance of this doctrine for Christians then and now. Bill and Gloria Gaither's song 'Because He lives, I can face tomorrow', written in 1970, encapsulates the importance of the resurrection for the believer.

Notes
[1]Edmund Clowney, *The Message of 1 Peter* (Nottingham: IVP, 1994)
I. Howard Marshall, *1 Peter* (Nottingham: IVP, 1991)

WEEK 6

Live Wisely

Opening Icebreaker

Make sure everyone has a small piece of paper – A6-sized would be good. Each person should write his or her name at the top and then pass it to the person on their left. This person should write on the bottom of the sheet an attitude that they have observed in the named person. The paper should then be folded from the bottom to hide the attitude and passed to the left again. After circulating the papers around the group, each person receives back their sheet, hopefully to be encouraged. No negative comments allowed!

Bible Readings

- 1 Peter 4:1–11
- John 13:1–17
- Romans 12:6–7
- Galatians 5:16–26
- 1 John 2:28; 4:7–12

Opening Our Eyes

A call to arms is issued at the start of Chapter 4:
the believer is encouraged to learn from the attitude
evidenced in Christ's suffering. The point is not that Jesus
is made stronger because He has endured temptation
and suffering, but that the attitude with which He faced
his sufferings should be shown in the lives of believers.
Attitude has often been described as an inward feeling
expressed by behaviour. Hence by observation one can
learn much about the attitude of another. John Maxwell
once said, 'Your attitude and your potential go hand in
hand'.[1] Christ suffered for our sinful disobedience on the
cross with an attitude demonstrating that sinful behaviour
must always be opposed and resisted.

Peter is aware that these believers had turned to Christ
from a variety of backgrounds and that now, having
received His grace and forgiveness, they needed to learn
to resist the pull of the past. The secret seems to be found
in dying to the sinful nature and allowing the victory
won by Christ to have free reign in their lives. Enough
time had been wasted in living in a way that grieved
God's heart and now they should live to please God. This
way of living would not be respected by all; in fact they
might receive abuse because they now wanted to live in
a different way. Living the Jesus way in an alien culture
is never easy – you might have discovered the reality of
that yourself! Peter says that there is a time coming when
we will all have to answer to God, who will judge every
person. So we have no need to be bothered about what is
falsely said about us right now, for it is God's assessment
that is all-important! It will always be difficult to share a
warning of the approaching judgment of God – it never
appeals to those who believe that death is final as this
gives them much more opportunity to live carelessly
whilst life lasts.

In the light of Christ's return and the end of all things, Christians are counselled to be alert and self-disciplined. An effective prayer life will only be possible if Christians are living in this God-honouring way. In terms of relationships within the body of believers, Christians should demonstrate the reality of their faith. The key characteristic is one of love that endures any amount of stretching and which can be lavished even on Christian brothers and sisters caught up in sinful behaviour. The same Greek word, used in verse 8 and 1:22, has the meaning of being at full stretch.

Living faithfully for Christ certainly made demands upon them and travelling Christian teachers often needed accommodation. The challenge was to offer assistance without begrudging it and with a right attitude. This gift of hospitality is one that Paul mentions in Romans 12:13 when talking about sincere love. Whatever gift we have been given by the Holy Spirit, we are called upon to exercise it for the mutual encouragement and blessing of our community. The key thing is that these spiritual gifts are gifts of grace, unearned or deserved and given 'for the common good' (1 Cor. 12:7; 14:12; Eph. 4:12). We are responsible for them being exercised for the wellbeing of others. These are service gifts which minister God's grace and bring praise to His name. They are to be used in His strength, with the end result of bringing God glory, not building the reputation of the user!

Discussion Starters

1. With the help of Philippians 2, seek to discover what the attitude of Christ was.

   _____

   _____

   _____

   _____

   _____

2. Can you remember a time when you were abused verbally for being a follower of Christ?

   _____

   _____

   _____

   _____

3. How would you open a conversation about the judgment to come? What do you think that judgment will mean for unbelievers?

   _____

   _____

   _____

   _____

   _____

4. What are you most looking forward to when Christ returns in glory?

   _____

   _____

   _____

   _____

5. Think about verse 6 and seek together to understand what Peter means.

_____

_____

_____

_____

_____

6. How can your love grow deep and be able to cover the indiscretions of others?

_____

_____

_____

_____

_____

7. What are your spiritual gifts? Help each other to recognise the spiritual gifts already received and think about ways that you can use them for the good of others.

_____

_____

_____

_____

_____

8. How important is it for Christians to develop a servant heart?

_____

_____

_____

_____

_____

Personal Application

For slaves or servants seeking to maintain a Christian witness, it was crucial to maintain a good attitude. Abused, ill-treated and ridiculed, their testimony could speak volumes. We are given to understand that some Roman homes were transformed by the powerful witness of slaves, committed to serving Christ in difficult situations. What opportunities do you have for sharing your faith? Do those around see tangible evidence of your faith? Are there ministries in your church to which God is calling you to be involved? Gifts given to all who love Jesus are for the blessing of others: are you taking responsibility for those given to you? Reread the lists in Romans 12, 1 Corinthians 12 and 14, and Ephesians 4:1–16, asking God to give you a servant heart so that you can be a blessing.

Seeing Jesus in the Scriptures

Peter wanted his readers to understand that persecution was not the end. It was inevitable that followers of Christ would be mistreated and abused; Jesus himself had warned His disciples of that possibility (John 15:18–25; 2 Tim. 3:12; Matt. 10:22). The good news was that He would be with them every step of the way to be their strength. Jesus had walked that way before them and endured the ignominy of the cross. Now, through the power of His Spirit, the fruits of His victory could be enjoyed in their everyday trials. There was also the joy of knowing that on His return, their troubles would pale into insignificance in the presence of His glory. However, until that day dawned, the call was to serve faithfully, ministering God's grace so that He would be praised.

Notes
[1] John Maxwell, *Attitude 101* (Nashville, Tennessee: Nelson, 2003) p13

WEEK 7

Ready to Serve Like Jesus

Opening Icebreaker

The picture of the shepherd is often used in the Bible but is increasingly less meaningful for urban dwellers. Think of an alternative which fits the twenty-first century and your personal situation. Share in the group the various pictures that are helpful today.

Bible Readings

- 1 Peter 5
- John 21:15–17
- Philippians 2:5–11
- 2 Thessalonians 2:16–17
- 2 Timothy 4:16–18
- Hebrews 13:5–8

Opening Our Eyes

John Stott suggests that 'to lead is to go ahead, to show the way and to inspire other people to follow.'[1] In this section, Peter sets out his own credentials for leadership and calls other leaders to serve like Jesus.

There is no attempt by Peter to stand on his apostolic credentials in verse 1. He is simply a 'fellow elder'. Notice how Peter plays down his authority; he is just one leader amongst others, but he is a witness to Christ's sufferings. Perhaps he wanted to remind his friends that the story of Christ's sufferings held many memories of failings of which he was not proud. He, like them, owed everything to the forgiving grace of God. He also mentions the hope of future glory and there is maybe a memory of a taste of that glory on the mountain, when Jesus was transfigured (Mark 9:2–8).

What are the qualifications necessary for church leadership? The first is that leaders function as shepherds, exercising tender loving care. Shepherds have three main functions; to lead their flock because they know the way; to feed them on fresh pasture and to protect the flock from predators. The word 'overseer' crops up again here (see 2:25), suggesting that the leader supportively watches over the progress and development of God's people.

The second qualification concerns the reasons for serving as a leader. Leading God's people is not something to do reluctantly, although nor is he advocating an arrogant gung ho approach. Often leaders struggle with their own frailties and inadequacy, but these traits often keep them humble and dependent on God's grace. There needs to be a clear sense of willingness and eagerness to serve, whilst responding to God's call. Finally Peter commands them that leaders are not to be consumed with a desire to build their own empires. Jesus, too, warned his disciples during

his earthly ministry not to be like worldly leaders
(Mark 9:33–37; 10:41–45).

Thirdly, Peter reminds them that humility is a crucial trait
to which leaders should aspire (vv5–6). Did he envisage
a leadership development programme in verse 5? These
younger men were encouraged to listen and learn from
those who were older and more experienced. Then a
word for all in the fellowship; live humbly with each
other. The word used here for 'clothe,' indicates a secure
tying on, perhaps as slaves did with their aprons.

All Christians should be aware that they are involved in
a battle (vv7–9). Anxiety can be handed over to Jesus
who longs to demonstrate His care. However we have
a responsibility to live soberly, which is far more than
just avoiding drunkenness; it demands that we are not
distracted from our hope. Peter no doubt remembered
the time in the garden when he slept instead of watching
with Jesus during his agony (Mark 14:37). Satan is
constantly at work in many disguises, trying to create
disunity and destruction. The Christ follower needs to be
ready to resist with a deep faith rooted in God, sure that
he or she is not alone in the fight.

The concluding doxology (vv10–11) is a prompt for
under-pressure Christians to be thankful that even if
they do suffer and maybe even fall short, they can have
confidence in 'the God of all grace'. This warm, pastoral
letter, which began with grace and peace, now concludes
with an encouragement too, not only to know the
theoretical doctrine, but to experience it in daily living.

Discussion Starters

1. Share with your group about someone who has demonstrated real leadership to you. Are there giftings that you recognise in that person that are spoken of here in 1 Peter?

   _____

   _____

   _____

   _____

   _____

2. What are the areas that most commonly cause Christian leaders to slip up? How can you help to support and care for your leaders?

   _____

   _____

   _____

   _____

   _____

3. Development of next generation leaders is crucial. What is your church doing to encourage new leaders?

   _____

   _____

   _____

   _____

   _____

4. It is easy to say, 'Cast all your anxiety on him' (v7), but what does this mean in reality? Share ways that have helped you to relieve anxiety.

   _____

   _____

   _____

   _____

   _____

5. How does the devil try to harass Christians? Are there any recent examples from your group which cause you concern? How can you help each other to resist him?

_____
_____
_____
_____
_____

6. Are you enjoying God's grace right now? Think of examples which will encourage others.

_____
_____
_____
_____
_____

7. Peter obviously delighted in the partnership of Silas and Mark. Who are the people who encourage you and how do they do that?

_____
_____
_____
_____
_____

8. Read through this chapter again and note the number of personal references that the writer makes, which would strongly indicate that the letter was written by Peter.

_____
_____
_____
_____
_____

Personal Application

Peter calls upon these Christians experiencing tough times to play their part in the development of the fledgling Church. Many were slaves or servants but they had been gifted by the Holy Spirit. Have you discovered your place in the body of Christ yet? Which gifts are you using and which are still in storage? How are you doing in your discipleship development? Look at the fruit of the Spirit (Gal. 5:22–26) and discern what is observable in you. How are you doing in the area of humility? Is there a growing depth of love for fellow believers? Is joy evident in your daily living? What else does Peter say about the fruit of the Spirit?

How could you encourage believers in other countries who are experiencing persecution? Are you regularly praying for them?

Seeing Jesus in the Scriptures

Devotion to Jesus is based on the facts that Jesus was promised, He came into this world to suffer and die for our sins, and His rising from the dead assures us that He has defeated Satan once and for all. We've received life-changing salvation through His work on the cross, but that is only the beginning and the expectation is that we are saved by His life, too (Romans 5:10). Scattered throughout the letter there are references to the return of the Lord Jesus (1:5,7,13; 4:13; 5:4). This doctrine always provides strength and hope for those living under pressure from persecution. So here the past, present and future tenses of salvation are employed by Peter as he seeks to minister to his struggling friends.

Notes
[1]John Stott, *Calling Christian Leaders* (Leicester: IVP, 2002)

Leader's Notes

Week 1: Good Reasons for Hope

Opening Icebreaker

The idea of this icebreaker is to stimulate our thinking about hope, starting with the basic hopes and anticipations that we possessed when we were quite young. Try not to dwell on hopes that were not realised but rather on confidence which was rewarded.

Aim of the Session

To encourage us to grow in our confidence in the promises of God and understand how we can also help others in this area.

Discussion Starters

1. This open question should help people to share what really hit them from the passage. You might like to start each discussion with this question, as it should encourage the group to open up and start talking.

2. This question focuses on verse 2 and may provide some interesting dialogue! Try not to stay just in the realm of the theoretical to work out ways of refuting cult members, although this verse is worth remembering for the future. Rather, concentrate on the practical implications of the Trinity and how the ministry of each member was important for Christians at the time Peter was writing and also for us today.

3. Prepare some passages from the Gospels and Acts such as Mark 8:27–33; 14:27–42,66–72, John 21 or Acts 10; the group will no doubt think of others, too. Trace how Jesus

never gave up on Peter and lavished His grace upon him throughout his life. Then share with others occasions when you have experienced special times of grace in your life and encourage others to share similarly.

4. Check out what Peter says to his friends about how they may maintain hope amidst tough times. Firstly you might like to look at the resurrection of Jesus, followed by a life of transforming faith and the anticipation of heaven. How have you found these reasons helpful when you have wanted to give up?

5. The story of Job is probably too long to read in its entirety, but use the suggested passages to focus your thoughts on his faith journey whilst being bombarded by unhelpful advice from his friends. What brought Job help in his agonising losses? How did he get to his declaration of faith in 42:1–5? How will you next try and help when a friend is struggling?

6. These verses contain an unexpected bonus for the reader! Think what they must have meant for a slave struggling with unjust suffering and abuse from an uncaring master. Going through tough times has the benefit of developing an increasing faith life. Have you ever experienced joy which is overwhelming and almost inexpressible? Joy always has a habit of showing itself on our faces!

7. Think about the implications of the resurrection of Jesus for your daily living. Which songs do you sing that pick up this thought? Maybe you could find a CD with the song being sung, which might help the group focus on the resurrection. You could also turn the song into a time of thanksgiving.

8. This is a tough question if people are struggling at the moment, but perhaps you could give an example from your life when you experienced joy in a dark time. Make sure that you don't take suffering lightly or trivialise its impact on your lives.

Week 2: Living as God's Holy People

Opening Icebreaker

This question will probably be straightforward for you and your integrity will shine through! However you might like to consider the effect of the temptation on someone younger in the faith, someone recently released from custody or someone praying for God to meet their immediate needs.

Aim of the Session

To discover what holiness means and how it may be evident in our daily lives without us being regarded as strange or weird.

Discussion Starters

1. The Church has often seemed to waiver between an overly intellectual approach to faith or an emotionally charged experiential one. The post-modern approach puts great weight on what you feel and experience. You may be able to detect the influences of this in your lives right now. Seek to help the group to understand that we need both approaches and that one is not better than the other, just different. How can we avoid the charge that as Christians we have thrown away our brains?

2. This question will require some thought and honesty from the group. Turn the discussion into prayer for each other.

3. How do you react to being called a foreigner and exile by Peter? Linking in to the second question, what do you think that it would mean for recipients of the letter and what does it mean for us today?

4. What are you afraid of? Talk about those things that bother you in life and try to understand what is being said here in relation to our attitude to our Father God. Writing in the sixteenth century, Martin Luther described experiencing a sort of terror in relation to God when he went to church. This may have been prompted by the pictures that adorned churches at that time which depicted God as a terrible judge. What pictures have influenced your thinking and how can you develop a right and helpful fear of God?

5. Share together helpful ways of memorising the Bible and think of times when verses came flooding back into your mind just when you needed them.

6. Discuss together ways of fostering love in relationships. Someone may have a personal example of this during a tough time which they were able to break through. These first century slaves often experienced unjust beatings; think what these words would have meant for them. How does this 'sincere love' relate to our work places or our homes?

7. The germs on which Paul Rees puts his finger in 2:1 are dangerous for a church or fellowship. Are you able to detect their presence in your group? And if so, how are you going to deal with them? It might be worth having a time of reflection at this point, asking God to reveal things that He is unhappy with and that need dealing with.

8. Think about a time in your family or with friends when a small baby demanded milk and then tucked into it almost without drawing a breath. How does this image help you when considering verses 2 and 3? Modern parents are particularly keen to keep records of development of their children. How can we chart progress in our spiritual lives?

Week 3: Chosen to Belong

Opening Icebreaker

This is your opportunity to use your imagination! Think about anything you have read about life in a royal home. There is an excellent book written by Queen Elizabeth II's cousin and childhood playmate, Margaret Rhodes, called *The Final Curtsey* which might help. Do you think this would be an experience you would like to have? If you want a biblical example, read 2 Samuel 9 and think about the experience of Mephibosheth.

Aim of the Session

To show something of the extent of God's amazing love for us and the plan that He had from before the beginning of time to build us into a body that demonstrates His life to the world around.

Discussion Starters

1. Imagine that a Christian was on trial for being a Christian. What sort of evidence would you expect to be submitted to the court by the prosecuting attorney? Think as a group about whether there would be enough evidence to convict you if you were in that position.

2. The Parable of the Tenants, as described by Matthew, quotes Psalm 118 just as Peter does in this passage and the story centres around the way that men and women reject the vineyard owner's son. It seems that in God's purposes the one rejected is the only one who can bring stability and hope to the world. Jesus is described as 'precious' and is crucial for God's building. How have you experienced His preciousness in your life?

3. We mentioned before that Peter quotes extensively from the Old Testament, yet often it is neglected by church groups, because it is sometimes regarded as hard to understand. As a group, consider the last message that you heard preached from the Old Testament. In what ways did it challenge your life?

4. First of all think through what these biblical phrases mean. Can you find other passages in the Bible that throw light upon their meaning? Perhaps you could try to find some twenty-first century equivalents that help them become more relevant to you. Try looking them up in a modern version or paraphrase. How do these phrases encourage you in your Christian life?

5. Everyone has struggles with living as a Christian in a world which is sometimes very alien. Consider together what you think would have been the main challenges for the Christians of Asia Minor at this time in history. Then spend some time considering the challenges you are facing at this time. What advice does Peter have that will help us make progress in our discipleship?

6. This is an opportunity for everyone to exercise the gift of encouragement! Consider your church and share the positive blessings that are evident at the moment. This would be a good moment to spend some time giving God praise for all He is doing. If you have a church leader present, pray for them too.

7. Sharing faith is never an easy task and evangelism is often regarded as being only the remit of extroverted people. Consider together how everyone can play their part in this crucial task. Sometimes we are so remote from the people we want to reach out to that they ignore our message. At other times we are so immersed in contemporary culture and so little different from them that we have nothing to say. Discuss how we can get the balance right and be effective for Jesus.

8. Think through what the word 'chosen' means to you. In Ephesians 1, Paul uses the word quite often and it does, of course, connect with that difficult word 'predestination'. You might want to encourage folk to go away and do some homework, to figure out why so much controversy has been engendered over the years by this word. Remember the often used illustration that a rowing boat needs two oars to keep it going straight!

Week 4: Now Give In!

Opening Icebreaker

This should spark some lively conversation for the group. If people are arguing both for and against striking, try to help them to see each other's side of the argument. Encourage them to understand that respect and honour are key issues here. You may decide that there could be circumstances that would cause you to lay down tools.

Aim of the Session

To show that respect and mutual submission are key elements in fostering healthy relationships. Also that submission to Christ as our leader is the starting point for all who claim to be His followers.

Discussion Starters

1. Here is an opportunity to discuss the role that authorities play in our lives. Note the key words 'God given', – if that is the case, we need to carefully examine our responses to them. Remember that it does not give those who rule over us the right to abuse the trust that we place in them or to act unjustly. You might like to think about appropriate action to take if laws were passed that were in direct opposition to God's regulations. This is a difficult topic and will need sensitivity.

2. What does it actually mean to respect others? Consider how you can do this without compromising your principles. What does God expect of us in this area? Can you gain some clues from the life of Jesus, especially in His last week on earth?

3. Think of recent examples of people who have hit the headlines because they were unwilling to compromise their principles. How can you support and encourage people whom you know in these circumstances? You might like to include them in some prayer support during the time you have together. If you have someone in the group who has suffered in this way it might be fitting to include them in your prayers.

4. If you have ever seen the film *The Passion of the Christ* you will be aware of the physical abuse and suffering that Jesus had to endure. As we know, His suffering touched more areas of life than that, as He struggled for the first time in eternity with being separated from His Father. In addition, there was the spiritual dimension of taking the punishment for our sinfulness. Imagine how that felt for one who was completely without sin! Think through what lessons you can learn from observing the way that Jesus faced up to suffering.

5. You may already mentor couples contemplating marriage or have been through a course yourselves. What are the key lessons you would like to emphasise from the passages mentioned 1 Peter 3:1–7, Ephesians 5:21–33 and Colossians 3:18–4:1?

6. Now you are really on difficult ground! Allow the conversation to flow as long as it is encouraging and affirming. This is not a time to embark on a battle of the sexes! See if you can tease out what Peter meant by 'weaker partner' – you may be sure he was not being condescending or patronising. The weakness being referred to by Peter is most likely to do with physicality, not spirituality.

7. Read 1 Peter 3:3–4. These verses say that 'beauty is in the eye of the beholder' but what sort of things identify someone as being beautiful? Don't get caught up with pointless discussions about whether a person should use make-up or visit an excellent hairdresser. Make time to encourage women in the group who display the loveliness of Christ.

8. Share together the things that hinder your prayer life. How can you help each other to grow and develop in this important area? A useful resource might be *Prayer Coach* by James L. Nicodem.

Week 5: Don't Let Suffering Take You by Surprise

Opening Icebreaker

As you discuss this subject there will be need for the leader to be really honest. If you are aware that someone else in the group has suffered for believing and that they would be willing to share, do prepare them for that role.

If there are no examples of this, search the internet on sites such as Barnabas Trust (barnabasfund.org) or Open Doors (opendoorsuk.org) and you should find some examples.

Aim of the Session

To help people understand that living for Christ will sometimes lead to big challenges and in the extreme, perhaps, a threat to life. Often the challenges we face are trivial compared to other brothers and sisters in other parts of the world.

Discussion Starters

1. First of all consider the difference between harmony and unison. The call most often in the New Testament is to harmony, where although we differ from one another we seek to find common ground. There is great strength in this approach as we do not expect everyone to be the same! Look at Philippians 1:27–2:11, in which Paul encourages a church to pull together. Are there clues in these two passages which could help us really live in harmony?

2. 'I'm ever so humble sir,' was the often repeated phrase of Uriah Heep in *David Copperfield* by Charles Dickens, yet none of us would aspire to be like him! Help the group work out what it means to be humble today. As some will no doubt struggle with self-worth issues you will need to take care in this discussion. Consider the quotation (sometimes attributed to C.S. Lewis) in the notes, which is important to remember. You might like to also consider what impact humility can have in the home and workplace.

3. Many people in Christian circles still have issues with fear. Again, people might like to share how they have found help in this area. Are there particular Bible verses which are useful, like 1 John 4:18 or 2 Timothy 1:7? Naming or acknowledging our fears sometimes loosens

their power over us. Spend some time praying for one another, and as leader remember your honesty will help and inspire the group.

4. The familiar verses in Isaiah 53 should be read as a group. Take time to consider how these words were fulfilled by Jesus when He went to the cross. Often we are taken up by the physical suffering of Jesus and that is clear here in this passage. Spend some time meditating on the mental and spiritual agony of Jesus' separation from His Father.

5. Peter encourages these first century Christians to be ready to share their faith (1 Pet. 3:15). You might like to consider what makes the story of a committed Christian effective in these times in which we live. Perhaps you could encourage people to share their story succinctly in about one or two minutes. One framework that people have used over the years is a 'before, at the time and after' structure. The emphasis should be upon how Jesus is working in my life right now!

6. Some in the group will have been baptised as Christian believers whilst others might have been baptised as small children. However, this is probably a good time to consider why we need to be baptised as part of God's family. Some might like to share the helpfulness of baptism to their Christian life and a DVD clip of a baptism might be appropriate.

7. Few would really be surprised that trials and struggles have been evident in their lives. How do we keep a right attitude when we are under pressure and how important is joy in helping us to do that? The group may have experiences which are well worth sharing. Beforehand, try to think through things that can help us during these times. Having a prayer partner, using an email to alert others to problems and memorising Bible verses may all play their part.

8. We talk much about God's faithfulness and there are many worship songs that pick up that theme. What does it mean when the going is tough? Many of these people being addressed were slaves; spend some time thinking about how they would have experienced His trustworthiness in their culture. Draw out stories from the group of when they have understood the power of this doctrine in their own lives.

Week 6: Live Wisely

Opening Icebreaker

This consequences-type exercise should bring encouragement to each member of the group. Give each person time to assimilate the attitudes observed by others in the group. This is when you identify the humble ones too! Make sure you discuss what an attitude is before you complete the exercise. An outward expression of an inner feeling – this is what you see in the behaviour of a person.

Aim of the Session

To show that effective Christian living presupposes a willing submission to God's will and purposes. It is never easy to live this way when things are tough and excuses are easy to find. We all need to ask ourselves some searching questions in order to discover whether we are truly living in a way pleasing to God.

Discussion Starters

1. Here is an opportunity to examine the attitude of Jesus as explained by Paul in Philippians 2 and compare it with what Peter says here in these verses. How did Jesus approach His earthly life and His death on the cross? The

eternal Son of God lived on earth, having left the glory of His Father's home and endured the abuse heaped on Him from the creatures He had made. Yet what does Peter say in chapter 2:21–24 about the way Jesus handled the attacks of others?

2. All of us seeking to live like Jesus will have to endure verbal abuse from others who want to make fun of our witness for Him. Often this is done through teasing and perhaps sometimes it is deserved because of our quirky ways. Try to help the group to be honest about how they are at home or at work. Be prepared to support and encourage those who have experienced abuse from others.

3. This is a tricky subject, especially if you want to win friends and influence people! Many people who are not yet committed Christians will have problems with this concept. It seems likely that Peter wanted to assure his fellow Christians who were suffering for their faith that those who were persecuting them would have to face God and give account of their actions at the return of Christ. Consider illustrations of where warnings are important for the preservation of life, for example, on a cliff top walk.

4. It might be useful to trace the number of times that Peter makes comment in this letter about the return of Christ. Encourage the group to share their thoughts and understanding of the implications of the return of Christ. Why are they looking forward to this amazing event?

5. Here is another difficult concept if we just take the verse 6 at face value. What is Peter hinting at here? Connections are often made with 3:19 but there are some obvious differences, especially in the two different Greek words used for preaching. The word in 3:19 is more 'proclamation', which is not always welcome, whilst in 4:6 the word relates to announcing good news. There is no hint anywhere else in the New Testament that there

is a doctrine of a second chance. This may have more
to do with the confusion in some believers' minds about
those believers who have already died – the gospel 'was'
preached to them whilst they were still alive. Hence they
are secure and their future is not in doubt.

6. Ask people in the group how they feel when they have
to deal with the indiscretions of another Christian. Does
verse 8 infer that sin does not really matter? Is 'covering
over' the equivalent of hiding things under the carpet?
Look at Proverbs 10:12. Perhaps Peter, who in answer to
his question in Matthew 18:21 was told that he was to
forgive his brother at least seventy-seven times, had really
taken that lesson to heart.

7. Read verses 9–11 once again and compare them with
Romans 12:3–8, 1 Corinthians 12–14 and Ephesians
4:1–16. If you have never undertaken a spiritual gifts
questionnaire this might be a good moment to do one;
you will find a number on the internet.[1] A simple exercise
would be to each use a piece of paper and repeat the
earlier exercise, this time recognising each other's spiritual
gifts. How will the people in your group use theirs to
bless and encourage others?

8. Much has been written over recent years about
developing a servant heart. Any conversation should look
first of all to the example of Jesus in the Gospels. Read
Mark 9:33–37, 10:35–45 and John 13:1–17. It is intriguing
that a number of respected leadership writers emphasise
this concept too. Robert Greenleaf writes: '… the great
leader is seen as a servant first, and that simple fact is the
key to [the leader's] greatness.'[2]

[1] A free download is available at www.cwr.org.uk/basicgift
[2] *Servant Leadership* (New York: Robert K. Greenleaf, Paulist Press, 1977) p7

Week 7: Ready to Serve Like Jesus

Opening Icebreaker

Be prepared with a number of alternative pictures which might be more appropriate than a shepherd for twenty-first century urban dwellers. Allow the group to offer suggestions of images that they would find helpful. If you live in a rural area it might be interesting to see whether the group still consider 'shepherd' to be a useful metaphor with which to work.

Aim of the Session

To encourage the group to engage in servant-hearted living and to understand it's importance in leadership in the local church.

Discussion Starters

1. Spend some time considering those who have been important in our lives and who have demonstrated effective biblical leadership. You could make a list of the traits that you would expect to see exercised in the church context. How does this list compare with what Peter shares in chapter 5? Be prepared for a lively discussion!

2. We read many examples in the media of where and how Christian ministers have failed and brought shame on God's name. It's easy to dismiss them as isolated incidents when often they are only the tip of the iceberg. The statistics do not make great reading, as many who start in Christian ministry do not finish well. Think of ways in which you can support and care for your leaders. Why not organise a surprise dinner party and write them 'thank you' cards?

3. Peter speaks in this chapter about young people (v5) and their need to have a submissive attitude. It could be

that an apprenticeship model of training was developing in the church of Peter's time. Certainly there is evidence of this from Paul's ministry and the way he nurtured Timothy and Titus. Here we read at the conclusion of the chapter of Peter's influence on Silas and Mark. How do we initially identify potential leaders in the church? How can we train and equip them for this crucial task?

4. Let's be honest – we all have times when anxiety overwhelms us! What do you think Peter meant by his command in verse 7? Again it is interesting to note that verses 6 and 7 form one sentence in the Greek and therefore a connection is made between humility and giving our worries back to God. The truly humble person who really lives for others may well be concerned about who will take care of them and thus will be anxious. Allow people to share how they have been helped in this area.

5. Again a difficult question to tackle! We need to avoid the twin polarities mentioned by C. S. Lewis in *Screwtape Letters*, namely that we often want to blame the devil for everything or ignore his reality altogether. Peter is sure that we are in a battle and that our enemy is dangerous. Some of his readers would already have witnessed the savagery of the lions in the amphitheatre. They needed to remember that lions hunt with great stealth as well as ferocious attack. Talk about how we can resist Satan's attacks and remember that the lion is tethered! See also James 4:7.

6. Grace is a beautiful word which is often used in the New Testament – you will know the definitions that are usually proposed. Start off by thinking about the grace of God shown in the sufferings of Christ to bring us forgiveness. The fact is that we are undeserving of His love and that there is nothing we have done which could have bought us entrance into His family. Allow members of the group to think of recent incidents in their lives when they have known the undeserved favour of God.

7. We all need people who will encourage us and cheer us on in our Christian journey. Peter, like Paul, worked in a team and obviously enjoyed the company of Silas and Mark. Are there people you think of with gratitude for their input into your life? We all need these people to encourage us and support us. If you detect that some in the group need this kind of fellowship you might need to think of ways in which this can be achieved.

8. This exercise should prove quite helpful. To get started, look at verse 1 where Peter speaks about being a 'witness of Christ's suffering' and verse 2, which might take you back to John 21. How much of the teaching here can you trace back to a saying of Jesus whilst on earth?

It might also be worth researching the link that is often made between Mark and Peter, and, in the light of verse 13, the influence Peter might have had on the narration of events in Mark's Gospel.

Cover to Cover Every Day
Gain deeper knowledge of the Bible

Each issue of these bimonthly daily Bible-reading notes gives you insightful commentary on a book of the Old and New Testaments with reflections on a psalm each weekend by Philip Greenslade.
Enjoy contributions from two well-known authors every two months and over a five-year period you will be taken through the entire Bible.

 **Individual issues available in epub/Kindle formats**

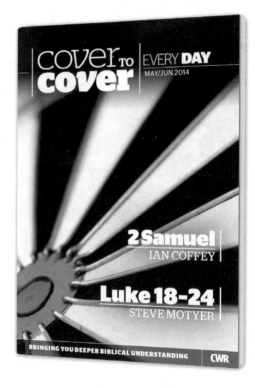

Cover to Cover Complete – NIV Edition
Read through the Bible chronologically

Take an exciting, year-long journey through the Bible, following
events as they happened.

- See God's strategic plan of redemption unfold across the centuries
- Increase your confidence in the Bible as God's inspired message
- Come to know your heavenly Father in a deeper way.

The full text of the NIV provides an exhilarating reading
experience and is augmented by our beautiful:

- Illustrations
- Maps
- Charts
- Diagrams
- Timeline

Key Scripture verses
and devotional thoughts
make each day's reading
more meaningful.

ISBN: 978-1-85345-804-0

Dramatic new resource

The Creed – Belief in action
by Phin Hall

What we believe shapes how we live, but what exactly do we believe as Christians? The Apostles' Creed exists to remind God's people about who He is and what He has done, and continues to do, for us.

72-page booklet, 210x148mm
ISBN: 978-1-78259-202-0

The bestselling *Cover to Cover* Bible Study Series

1 Corinthians
Growing a Spirit-filled church
ISBN: 978-1-85345-374-8

2 Corinthians
Restoring harmony
ISBN: 978-1-85345-551-3

1 Peter
Good reasons for hope
ISBN: 978-1-78259-088-0

1 Timothy
Healthy churches –
effective Christians
ISBN: 978-1-85345-291-8

23rd Psalm
The Lord is my shepherd
ISBN: 978-1-85345-449-3

2 Timothy and Titus
Vital Christianity
ISBN: 978-1-85345-338-0

Acts 1-12
Church on the move
ISBN: 978-1-85345-574-2

Acts 13-28
To the ends of the earth
ISBN: 978-1-85345-592-6

Barnabas
Son of encouragement
ISBN: 978-1-85345-911-5

Bible Genres
Hearing what the Bible really says
ISBN: 978-1-85345-987-0

Daniel
Living boldly for God
ISBN: 978-1-85345-986-3

Ecclesiastes
Hard questions and
spiritual answers
ISBN: 978-1-85345-371-7

Elijah
A man and his God
ISBN: 978-1-85345-575-9

Ephesians
Claiming your inheritance
ISBN: 978-1-85345-229-1

Esther
For such a time as this
ISBN: 978-1-85345-511-7

Fruit of the Spirit
Growing more like Jesus
ISBN: 978-1-85345-375-5

Galatians
Freedom in Christ
ISBN: 978-1-85345-648-0

Genesis 1-11
Foundations of reality
ISBN: 978-1-85345-404-2

God's Rescue Plan
Finding God's fingerprints
on human history
ISBN: 978-1-85345-294-9

Great Prayers of the Bible
Applying them to our lives today
ISBN: 978-1-85345-253-6

Hebrews
Jesus – simply the best
ISBN: 978-1-85345-337-3

Hosea
The love that never fails
ISBN: 978-1-85345-290-1

Isaiah 1-39
Prophet to the nations
ISBN: 978-1-85345-510-0

Isaiah 40-66
Prophet of restoration
ISBN: 978-1-85345-550-6

James
Faith in action
ISBN: 978-1-85345-293-2

Jeremiah
The passionate prophet
ISBN: 978-1-85345-372-4

John's Gospel
Exploring the seven miraculous signs
ISBN: 978-1-85345-295-6

Joseph
The power of forgiveness and reconciliation
ISBN: 978-1-85345-252-9

Judges 1-8
The spiral of faith
ISBN: 978-1-85345-681-7

Judges 9-21
Learning to live God's way
ISBN: 978-1-85345-910-8

Mark
Life as it is meant to be lived
ISBN: 978-1-85345-233-8

Moses
Face to face with God
ISBN: 978-1-85345-336-6

Names of God
Exploring the depths of God's character
ISBN: 978-1-85345-680-0

Nehemiah
Principles for life
ISBN: 978-1-85345-335-9

Parables
Communicating God on earth
ISBN: 978-1-85345-340-3

Philemon
From slavery to freedom
ISBN: 978-1-85345-453-0

Philippians
Living for the sake of the gospel
ISBN: 978-1-85345-421-9

Prayers of Jesus
Hearing His heartbeat
ISBN: 978-1-85345-647-3

Proverbs
Living a life of wisdom
ISBN: 978-1-85345-373-1

Revelation 1-3
Christ's call to the Church
ISBN: 978-1-85345-461-5

Revelation 4-22
The Lamb wins! Christ's final victory
ISBN: 978-1-85345-411-0

Rivers of Justice
Responding to God's call to righteousness today
ISBN: 978-1-85345-339-7

Ruth
Loving kindness in action
ISBN: 978-1-85345-231-4

The Covenants
God's promises and their relevance today
ISBN: 978-1-85345-255-0

The Creed
Belief in action
ISBN: 978-1-78259-202-0

The Divine Blueprint
God's extraordinary power in ordinary lives
ISBN: 978-1-85345-292-5

The Holy Spirit
Understanding and experiencing Him
ISBN: 978-1-85345-254-3

The Image of God
His attributes and character
ISBN: 978-1-85345-228-4

The Kingdom
Studies from Matthew's Gospel
ISBN: 978-1-85345-251-2

The Letter to the Colossians
In Christ alone
ISBN: 978-1-85345-405-9

The Letter to the Romans
Good news for everyone
ISBN: 978-1-85345-250-5

The Lord's Prayer
Praying Jesus' way
ISBN: 978-1-85345-460-8

The Prodigal Son
Amazing grace
ISBN: 978-1-85345-412-7

The Second Coming
Living in the light of Jesus' return
ISBN: 978-1-85345-422-6

The Sermon on the Mount
Life within the new covenant
ISBN: 978-1-85345-370-0

The Tabernacle
Entering into God's presence
ISBN: 978-1-85345-230-7

The Ten Commandments
Living God's Way
ISBN: 978-1-85345-593-3

The Uniqueness of our Faith
What makes Christianity distinctive?
ISBN: 978-1-85345-232-1

For current prices or to order visit www.cwr.org.uk/store
Available online or from Christian bookshops.

Courses and seminars

Publishing and media

Conference facilities

Transforming lives

CWR's vision is to enable people to experience personal transformation through applying God's Word to their lives and relationships.
Our Bible-based training and resources help people around the world to:
• Grow in their walk with God
• Understand and apply Scripture to their lives
• Resource themselves and their church
• Develop pastoral care and counselling skills
• Train for leadership
• Strengthen relationships, marriage and family life and much more.
Our insightful writers provide daily Bible-reading notes and other resources for all ages, and our experienced course designers and presenters have gained an international reputation for excellence and effectiveness.
CWR's Training and Conference Centres in Surrey and East Sussex, England, provide excellent facilities in idyllic settings – ideal for both learning and spiritual refreshment.

CWR Applying God's Word
to everyday life and relationships

CWR, Waverley Abbey House,
Waverley Lane, Farnham,
Surrey GU9 8EP, UK

Telephone: +44 (0)1252 784700
Email: info@cwr.org.uk
Website: www.cwr.org.uk

Registered Charity No 294387
Company Registration No 1990308

NATIONAL DISTRIBUTORS

UK: (and countries not listed below)
CWR, Waverley Abbey House, Waverley Lane, Farnham, Surrey GU9 8EP.
Tel: (01252) 784700 Outside UK (44) 1252 784700

AUSTRALIA: KI Entertainment, Unit 21 317-321 Woodpark Road, Smithfield, New South Wales 2164. Tel: 1 800 850 777 Fax: 02 9604 3699. Email: sales@kientertainment.com.au

CANADA: David C Cook Distribution Canada, PO Box 98, 55 Woodslee Avenue, Paris, Ontario N3L 3E5. Tel: 1800 263 2664 Email: joy.kearley@davidccook.ca

GHANA: Challenge Enterprises of Ghana, PO Box 5723, Accra.
Tel: (021) 222437/223249 Fax: (021) 226227 Email: ceg@africaonline.com.gh

HONG KONG: Cross Communications Ltd, 1/F, 562A Nathan Road, Kowloon.
Tel: 2780 1188 Fax: 2770 6229 Email: cross@crosshk.com

INDIA: Crystal Communications, Plot No. 125, Road No.7, T.M.C, Mahendra Hills, East Marredpally, Secunderabad - 500026 Tel/Fax: (040) 27737145
Email: crystal_edwj@rediffmail.com

KENYA: Keswick Books and Gifts Ltd, PO Box 10242-00400, Nairobi.
Tel: (020) 2226047/312639 Email: sales.keswick@africaonline.co.ke

MALAYSIA: Canaanland Distributors Sdn Bhd, No. 25 Jalan PJU 1A/41B, NZX Commercial Centre, Ara Jaya, 47301 Petaling Jaya, Selangor. Tel: (03) 7885 0540/1/2 Fax: (03) 7885 0545 Email: info@canaanland.com.my

Salvation Publishing & Distribution Sdn Bhd, 23 Jalan SS 2/64, 47300 Petaling Jaya, Selangor. Tel: (03) 78766411/78766797 Fax: (03) 78757066/78756360
Email: info@salvationbookcentre.com

NEW ZEALAND: KI Entertainment, Unit 21 317-321 Woodpark Road, Smithfield, New South Wales 2164, Australia. Tel: 0 800 850 777 Fax: +612 9604 3699
Email: sales@kientertainment.com.au

NIGERIA: FBFM, Helen Baugh House, 96 St Finbarr's College Road, Akoka, Lagos. Tel: (+234) 01-7747429, 08075201777, 08186337699, 08154453905
Email: fbfm_1@yahoo.com

PHILIPPINES: OMF Literature Inc, 776 Boni Avenue, Mandaluyong City.
Tel: (02) 531 2183 Fax: (02) 531 1960 Email: gloadlaon@omflit.com

SINGAPORE: Alby Commercial Enterprises Pte Ltd, 95 Kallang Avenue #04-00, AIS Industrial Building, 339420. Tel: (65) 629 27238 Fax: (65) 629 27235
Email: marketing@alby.com.sg

SOUTH AFRICA: Life Media & Distribution, Unit 20, Tungesten Industrial Park, 7 C R Swart Drive, Strydompark 2125 Tel: (+27) 0117924277 Fax: (+27) 0117924512 Email: orders@lifemedia.co.za

SRI LANKA: Christombu Publications (Pvt) Ltd, Bartleet House, 65 Braybrooke Place, Colombo 2. Tel: (+941) 2421073/2447665. Email: christombupublications@gmail.com

USA: David C Cook Distribution Canada, PO Box 98, 55 Woodslee Avenue, Paris, Ontario N3L 3E5, Canada. Tel: 1800 263 2664. Email: joy.kearley@davidccook.ca

For email addresses, visit the CWR website: www.cwr.org.uk
CWR is a Registered Charity - Number 294387
CWR is a Limited Company registered in England - Registration Number 1990308